The Social, Economic and Political Impacts of Direct Trade Coffee Production in Santa Barbara, Honduras—

From Farmlevel to Streetlevel

By Katherine Slocum

Professor Moodie, Advisor

Anthropology Department

University of California, Santa Cruz

2015

VERVE

Katie and Juan Benitez

Table of Contents

It took ten years in the coffee industry before I tasted my first red, ripe coffee cherry fresh off the tree. This wasn't any coffee cherry, either. Juan Benitez's fruit was rich and complex. I tasted banana, papaya, the rubber of the skin, the slick mucilage clinging to the green beans nestled within the cherry exterior. At 4500 feet, the humid equatorial air had grown thinner, enshrouding the mountainside in a tenuous gray cloud, and I shivered as the mid-afternoon sun was obscured. Around me, a buzzing chorus of hidden exotic birds' sudden chirps rang, along with the occasional chortle from Juan Benitez's free-roaming horse, the laughter and barefoot romping of his children, curious about the visitors wandering their farm, and the intermittent hacking of his machete as he trolled the manicured aisles of coffee, eliminating weeds. Far off in the distance below gleamed the surface of Lago de Yojoa, where we were staying at night after days of trucking it up the steep mountain.

I was 24-years-old, standing on that slope because I had decided to synergistically combine my passion for coffee, my calling to help people, and my pursuit of a degree in anthropology. What if I could examine the commercial way coffee is usually purchased worldwide in comparison to a more specialized boutique process called "direct trade" in the hopes of theorizing a more socially just life for farmers and producers along the supply chain of the second-most traded commodity globally? Then a paradox occurred to me: while much higher specialty coffee prices are alluring for farmers living in impoverished nations dependent upon on export crops, what happens when catastrophe strikes, fungus ravages their plants, or they can't tend to their farms, and they don't get paid for their crops? What does the neocolonial dynamic of top-down market-based solutions to a commodity crop mean ethically for all parties involved?

Coffee is at its roots a colonial crop, cultivated by the lineages of slaves—held by the English, French, Dutch, Spanish and American—and exported to the imperial centers to fuel the elite and sate the Euro-American masses, propelling them into fully productive members of an industrializing society. Like all farming, it is an inherently risky enterprise, especially for subsistence farmers whose livelihood depends upon the contingent compensation of benefactors from the Global North. The concept of benevolently assisting farmers in the Global South, whose crops are highly susceptible to environmental destruction, hangs in a matrix of ethical ambiguity.

Standing on Juan Benitez's farm, exactly one year had elapsed since a local coffee roaster in Santa Cruz called Verve had hired me. When I first met Colby Barr, the co-owner and green buyer, he had emphasized that not only does Verve strive for quality, it demands it, and offers farmers who can produce high-grown specialty coffee a premium for their product. He claimed to have spent 225% more than market value for the coffee he purchased in 2012. Sounds crazy. Even crazier, the model was proving lucrative for the burgeoning business. Colby asked my group of new hires to help him find a way to better connect producers ("farmlevel") and customers ("streetlevel"), the two ends of a supply chain spanning thousands of miles, and as many hands of the integral humans involved along every step. It was at that moment that the seed was planted for me to write an ethnography about Verve's coffee purchasing process (specifically in Honduras), focusing on the economic, social and political effects direct trade has on producers, their families, and the people along the supply chain.

Placing it in a larger cultural context, what is specialty coffee, "direct trade", and "third wave coffee"? How is this different from how coffee is sold and purchased under fair trade and commercially on the "C" Coffee Commodity market? How do environmental factors, such as an airborne fungus rust, called "roya", impact producers and their profits? Who backs the farmer up when those environmental factors wipe out an entire crop?

Verve's philosophy is intricate and multifaceted, but its main feature is fostering an ongoing relationship with farmers to promote sustainable buying practices. How do those relationships form? How do they evolve, growing season by growing season? And what happens when one party doesn't hold up their end of the commitment? Verve's profit model has only been in place for seven years, and during that time it has experienced great material returns on its investments, which landed it hundreds of new wholesale accounts, carrying the brand worldwide. It has also received accolades like barista competition titles and the Good Food Award two years running which underscore its priority of coffee and service quality. Given that success, the company has begun to expand. With that expansion comes the possibility to provide more producers with a higher wage. Yet, how will the growth affect the system? Will the ratio remain intact? Using Santa Cruz based coffee company Verve Coffee Roasters as a case study, I will examine the direct trade method in juxtaposition with commercial and fair trade coffee, analyzing the costs and benefits of each.

Fair trade has pervaded society as a means of consumer redemption, that guilt-erasing mechanism that consumers employ to feel they are voting for conscious products with their dollars. Yet, many scholars, including Sarah Lyon, Daniel Reichmann, Julia

Smith, David Jaffe, and Molly Doane, have called into question the actual fairness of the system as the demands grow increasingly challenging for farmers to meet. Since the collapse of the International Coffee Agreement in 1989, producers have experienced the unpredictability and uncertainty of plummeting and skyrocketing fluctuations in the price of coffee set by the "C" market. Direct trade can alleviate that pressure, and provide extra money and resources for producers who meet the criteria, increasing quality of life and access to a more socially just supply chain without exploitation or estrangement. However, telescoping down to the farmers I interacted with, whose farms are all on the same slope of one mountain in Honduras, each has received more money for their product, but still live in a country with little to no infrastructure, with children to feed and clothe, and plants that are vulnerable to roya unless meticulous, back-breaking care is tended to their plants daily. Some have experienced great success, and have been awarded accolades such as the Cup of Excellence for their coffee. Others can't adjust to the farming, nutrition and grooming actions necessary to keep up with the demand of a direct trade relationship.

Though direct trade seems like a more viable option to the commercial system's volatility, there remains another capriciousness in the possibility that vendors like Verve won't be able to purchase the farmer's crop, despite an established relationship, due to such variables as environmental destruction, drought, lack of maintenance, or lower cupping scores, all of which are not outside of the realm of possibility season to season. What are independent farmers' alternative options if a system like direct trade fails and they've disqualified themselves from fair trade, which requires membership in a co-op? Some Honduran producers harvests are so late that no mills are open by the time they're willing to sell. What options would producers have if Verve decided not to purchase? Is there a viable solution that provides farmers with more job security and reassurance that, despite outlying factors, they can rely on a livable wage as seasons pass? Is there a way to grant farmers a more democratic voice in how their coffee is purchased, instead of hoping that once-a-year visitors like Verve will choose their crop to fund?

Chapter One

The Colonial Origins and Continuance of Coffee as a Global Commodity

It is estimated that 125 million people worldwide depend on coffee farming to sustain their livelihood[1]. Coffee is consumed by millions of people worldwide. The small plant only produces an average of one pound of coffee per year, yet it has found a way to permeate our everyday lives. Coffee is only grown in the regions between the Tropic of Cancer and the Tropic of Capricorn, in countries that line the equator. It is only grown in Latin America, Africa, and Asia. The only American state that produces coffee is Hawaii, but its yield only accounts for 6-7 million pounds on average compared to 12 billion produced globally. Brazil produces the most coffee of any country, 40% with over five billion pounds, but that is due to the fact that most of the coffee it exports is the robusta species, which is characterized by smaller, less flavorful beans. The most desirable, and most frequently grown, bought and sold species of coffee is called arabica. Among arabica and robusta there are several

[1] Fair Trade and Coffee Commodity Briefing 2012, Fairtrade.net

different varieties of coffee. Some examples include yellow and red catuai, bourbon, pacamara, SL-28, SL-34, caturra, gesha, pacas, typica and many more. Similar to wine grapes (how there are varieties like pinot noir, cabernet sauvignon, syrah) these variations occur due to breeding, cross-pollination, geographical location and genetic modifications. Also like wine, each variety tastes different and exhibits different characteristics. Every variable factor changes the flavor of coffee in some way; country of origin, elevation, soil conditions (terroir), weather, farming practices, processing, milling, roasting, and more all influence the taste of a coffee.

The story of how coffee rose to prominence begins with the legendary goat herder named Kaldi in Ethiopia whose goats suddenly gained a lot of ecstatic energy after nibbling berries from a tall bush[2]. Kaldi himself sampled the cherries and realized they contain two seeds, covered in a slick skin, which give the consumer a little boost. It was taken from Ethiopia to the Yemeni province of Arabia, and the Arabs were the first to trade coffee. By the 16th century, it had reached Persia, Egypt, Syria and Turkey. Word began to spread to Europe of the curious beverage when travelers would pass through the Orient. This was during the rise in prominence of

---

[2] National Coffee Assocation, ncasua.org, "The History of Coffee"

other exotic imports like tobacco, chocolate and tea, and once coffee reached Europe, it became a luxury for the elite.

In the German historian Wolfgang Schivelbush's history of social stimulants, *Tastes of Paradise,* he chronicles this lineage and says, "By about 1700 it was firmly established as a beverage, not, of course, for the entire population but certainly among the trend-setting strata of society" (Schivelbush 1992:19). It was credited as a cure-all for virtually any disorder, disease or illness, and soon was revered for its sobering capacities. Some people warned against its undesirable effects, and others neutrally observed its artificial enhancement of alertness. The schema was set for coffee to be consumed first thing in the morning. Soon, coffeehouses started popping up almost as ubiquitously as Starbucks would centuries later. "According to documents from the period, around 1700 there were some 3,000 coffeehouses in London. With a population of 600,000 that would have meant one coffeehouse for every 20 people...Exaggerated though the figure 3,000 may be, the fact remains that the coffeehouse played a central role during this period when London was the international hub of capitalism" (51).

Like the salons of the Enlightenment that would soon appear, coffeehouses became known as congregation spaces for political and literary conversations, where people from different backgrounds would sip coffee, read the newspaper and eat pastries. Writers would meet journalists and financiers, patrons of the art to perhaps storyboard ideas, while perhaps lawyers would stop by to fuel up before parliament.

Yet, all of this, in conjunction with the high taxes placed on luxuries like coffee, ensured that it remained a treat for the elite, and coffee became a highly coveted object of colonial exploitation. "As coffee could not be cultivated in cold northern latitudes, it was a natural product for the colonial division of labor, entirely produced in tropical colonies, transported on metropolitan ships, reexported to countries without colonies of their own, and mainly consumed in the West" (Clarence-Smith and Topik[1] 2003:6).[3] Meanwhile, in Brazil, where most of the world's coffee is produced, the production depended upon the labor of slaves. In Latin America, colonial rulers forced indigenous peoples into coffee production. "Mayans were forced into the coffee fields of Guatemala and Mexico, whereas in Nicaragua, market forces proved stronger than coercion in coaxing Amerindians and others to participate in the coffee economy" (9). The Portuguese colonies, namely Brazil, didn't solve the forced labor

---

[3] William Gervase Clarence-Smith and Stephen Topik were co-editors of the comprehensive analysis of the history of coffee from 1500-1989 entitled *The Global Coffee Economy in Africa, Asia and Latin America*

issue until the early 1960s. Similarly, French colonies did not abolish forced labor until the end of WWII.

Sidney Mintz is an anthropologist whose work revolves around the slave trade and production of sugar and coffee in the Caribbean during the 17th and 18th centuries. His theory is that the Caribbean, with its influx of multicultural slaves and imperial pressure to produce sugar and coffee, actually modernized before the Global North did.[4] Colonial forces used the labor of their slaves to accelerate the global proliferation of coffee as an aid to keep their workforce attentive and alert as the world began to industrialize. Coffee and sugar became ammunition in the conversion of the workforce into assembly-line manufacturing and the mechanized 12-hour work shifts.

It was through the Caribbean channel that Mintz focuses on that coffee was promulgated into Central and South America by the colonizers who brought the plants with them. Its epicenter was Martinique in 1720, and from there it spread to Mexico, Haiti and Brazil. Earliest records show that coffee must have appeared in Honduras in 1804.[5] Despite this early arrival, Honduran coffee

---

4 "Enduring Substances, Trying Theories: The Caribbean Region as *Oikoumene*" Sidney Mintz, 1996

5 Honduran Coffee Institute, quoting the Statistical Yearbook of Honduras of 1889-1893

production was not considered important in the grand scheme of the coffee market until the 1950s. The economy of Honduras long relied on bananas as its main export crop but during and after WWII, banana demand and prices plummeted, delivering a devastating blow to the workers and families who grew them. Attention turned to coffee as a cash crop and numbers of production began to rise. Today, Honduras is the second most productive country in Central America, producing over 350 million pounds in 2014, trailing Guatemala by almost 50%.

Daniel Reichman illuminates this increase and foreshadows the impact of the International Coffee Agreement in his book about coffee in Honduras, *The Broken Village*, "The coffee sector in Honduras experienced dramatic growth in the 1970s and 1980s, supported by development aid from the U.S. Agency for International Development (USAID). During this period, coffee was regulated by the International Coffee Agreement (ICA), a treaty that established a governing body, the International Coffee Organization (ICO) to control the production and sale of coffee to and from its member countries...Price control was the major function of the ICO" (Reichman 2011: 47-48). The symbol of the ICA represents precisely the unequal footing on which farmers and consumers are standing, when a powerful institution from the Global North is instrumental in the success of developing nations. As Reichman goes on to explain, the ICA was a blessing and a curse.

The ICA guaranteed a price minimum as a means of ameliorating the perennial risk that farmers experience in investing their lives in cash crops, yet the agreement hinged on a quota system, which Honduras would often far exceed. This excessive production was a violation of the treaty's terms and would force prices down. The ICO and the ICA still exist, but there was a termination of a current agreement in 1989. Since then there have been more iterations, the most recent being in 2007, but Reichman discusses the fallout of the 1989 termination. "Despite the many flaws in the ICA system, on the whole, it prevented wild swings in prices that have occurred since its demise. It offered a mechanism to control the cyclical volatility that could lead to social unrest in coffee-growing regions. For small producers who value economic security over the potential for high profits, the ICA system was an important safety net" (48).

The collapse of a system that mitigated risk for Honduran farmers led to the producers and buyers within the market looking for alternative systems to the commercial way coffee is bought and sold.

On average, Americans drink one cup of coffee per day, and it is used in every social context, from breakfast drink/eye-opener, study aid, first date catalyst, road trip necessity, and sobering up device. Cafes are a staple in our cultural landscape. King among them, in terms of presence and monopoly, is giant megacorporation Starbucks, which has over 21,000 stores in 66 countries. In 2012, a cartographic study was released to show that every American is within at most 170 miles of a Starbucks anywhere in the country[6]. Of course, many of those are much closer distances from one another, and the "one on every corner" cliché is very true in some metropolitan cities. Corporate giants like Starbucks, and to a lesser degree, Peet's and homebrew companies like Folger's and Nescafe utilize the "C" Market as a determination of price for the massive amounts of beans they buy. The "C" or Coffee market is a commodity trading market where investors and speculators trade based on the value price of coffee in a commercial sense. This means that coffee, like oil, wheat, corn, and various agricultural goods, including animals, are exchanged based on a future predicted price. In America, this takes place in the New York Board of Trade

---

[6] Jim Davenport, University of Washington PhD candidate, 2012, http://www.ifweassume.com/2012/10/the-united-states-of-starbucks.html

(NYBOT) and is traded under the symbol C or KC. This price becomes the price that is used to determine fair trade floor and also the price that specialty coffee uses to determine their premium prices.

Just as Mintz intimated in his survey of industrialized sugar and coffee production, the world has grown accustomed to this daily drink from far away equatorial countries, and the mass-marketed corporate-branded cups easily accessible to us on every corner have cast a mirage over the exploitation and neocolonialism that takes place at origin every day. Producers work to exhaustion, against the threat of environmental or other disasters, to meet the demands of a volatile commercial market. With the ICA in and out of flux, integral players in and outside of the production chain began to look for alternatives.

CHAPTER TWO:

FAIR TRADE AS A SOLUTION?

As a response to the market volatility and the collapse of the ICA, the coffee industry searched for an alternative to the C market and its ups and downs. "The abandonment of longstanding multilateral efforts to regulate commodity prices, such as the International Coffee Agreement (ICA)...has also forced producer prices for many commodities to unprecedented lows...By the 1990s, coffee growers experienced the lowest prices in a generation, and the decade witnessed deepening material hardship and even starvation in some coffee-growing regions" (Lyon & Moberg 2010:3). As the editors of a book of social science essays on the effects of fair trade, *Fair Trade and Social Justice*, Lyon and Moberg cite neoliberal globalization as a pressurizing effect that catalyzed fair trade's arrival in the market, as an attempt to alleviate pressure and revitalize the market for struggling producers. Fair trade seeks to give equilibrium to production, labor, environmental impact and price ceilings and has become a social justice mechanism championing disadvantaged producers, artisans and craftswomen usually in the global south, and coffee farmers are included under that vast umbrella.

Yet, like many of their contemporaries, Lyon and Moberg are skeptical of Fair Trade due to the controversies that have arisen since its introduction to the market. Many scholars are wary of the top-down dynamics between producers involved in Fair Trade, the oftentimes well-meaning consumer activist at the other end, and the corroded supply chain in between. As popularity for Fair Trade consumption has reached its apex, so too has the duplicitous nature of Fair Trade marketing to entice consumers who seek redemption through more socially beneficial choices. Companies like Starbucks, Tom's "1-for-1" shoes, (RED) campaign, myriad retailers of chocolate, tea, coffee, flowers, cotton, hemp—the list goes on—have carved out a niche market that relies on and is exponentially successful because of the consumer activism and redemption that it promises: By buying our stuff, you're helping the world, and you'll feel better about buying it!

This is what philosopher and cultural critic Slavoj Žižek refers to as "cultural capitalism" in his lecture "First as Comedy, Then as Farce" delivered in 2009 for an event for The Royal Society for the Encouragement of Arts, Manufactures and Commerce in London. He points out the inherent hypocrisy in a paradox like charitable business, saying that, "You don't just buy a coffee you buy in the very consumerist act—you buy your redemption from being only a consumerist" (RSA). While he commiserates with the very human reaction to see suffering in the world and to want to fix it, even if that means using your dollar to be an activist in some small way. He argues that this doesn't fix the problem but rather prolongs it. Žižek calls out Tom's as a company that is utilizing consumer activism to apply a bandage to a social problem by issuing shoes to those "in need," circumventing the real bureaucratic boundaries and social inequities, all while making a huge profit.

One of Fair Trade's controversies is the rigid and complicated third-party certification system. To be involved in fair trade, membership is safeguarded by a rigorous certification process, which must be performed by a third party, such as Fair Trade International or Fairtrade Labeling Organizations International (FLO). Certification criteria can be overwhelming for farmers to meet, and some scholars argue it is akin to the high expectations of specialty coffee, minus the premium prices. Lyon and Moberg also assert that,

> The contemporary fair trade movement rests on a deep (and perhaps deepening) paradox. Many consumers of fair trade goods are motivated by a strenuous opposition to the effects of neoliberal globalization as measured in the growing poverty and environmental damage in many regions of the developing world. In seeking social justice and

> environmental sustainability, however, fair trade pursues a market-based solution to the very problems developing from free markets (7).

As mentioned, coffee prices have been known to plummet to as low as 42 cents per pound (the record low in October 2001)[7]. Right now, fair trade guarantees a floor price of $1.40, and $1.70 for organic fair trade coffee. This ensures that, even if the coffee market falls to record lows, those growers with fair trade certified coffee would still be able to sell their coffee for $1.40. If the market goes up, the fair trade price mirrors it.

The certification processes for fair trade coffee are arduous, and the third party certification agents set standards that make producing fair trade coffee expensive. In her ethnographic article published in Lyon and Moberg's book, Julia Smith argues that fair trade's qualifications have made for challenging criteria for farmers to meet. "The end result is that while the price paid to fair trade producers has remained nearly constant, falling behind when inflation is taken into account, the costs involved in producing fair trade coffee have continually risen" (Smith 2010:35). Fair trade is more of a viable option for farmers as a preventative failsafe for

---

[7] tradingeconomics.com coffee |1972-2015|

when coffee prices are low, but the cost of production and the intense scrutiny by certification agencies makes it difficult for growers to break even. In addition, in order to be certified fair trade, farmers have to be members of co-ops, and, because co-ops sometimes require single-origin coffees to be melded together in blends and sold as one unit, it can be more lucrative to sell independently, even with the associated risks.

In her ethnography of the coffee industry in Papua New Guinea, Paige West lays out the labors of coffee production in juxtaposition with the compensation the farmer receives after the bean has been through the harvesting, milling, drying, hulling, sorting and exporting processes of the supply chain. West begins her narrative by assessing consumer behavior and their choices. She says that which coffee we choose to buy is fueled by a political ecology, manipulated by the media and markets. "People who refuse to drink Starbucks coffee may think they are sending a message of opposition to large corporations that they imagine are putting mom-and-pop or individually owned establishments out of business. Those who always buy fair-trade coffee may be trying to send the message that they care about the plight of rural farmers in the tropics" (West 2012)[8]. In West's narrative is echoed the consumer redemption sentiments laid out by Žižek wherein consumers use their dollars to vote for what they believe is the more just product.

Daniel Reichmann's ethnography about coffee growers in Honduras adds to this concept of buying for the perceived greater good. He calls it the "Ethical Consumption Model" and "the opposite of the boycott. Rather than calling for a prohibition of certain goods, this type of action calls for consumers to purchase products that conform to a particular set of values...In these cases, individual choices are interpreted as political acts, but this acts do not communicate a message outward" (Reichmann 2011:149). Not only is Fair Trade perhaps masquerading behind consumer activism to create immense wealth for Global Northern businesses, there are fallacies and contradictions within the system. Debarati Sen's essay "Fair Trade Organic Tea Production and Women's Poltical Futures in Darjeeling, India" seeks to expose the hierarchies and institutional structures within that region's tea co-ops and exploitation and capitalization on their female workers' imposed ignorance. "In the plantation, the strict bureaucratic hierarchy, top-down obedience structure, and corrupt labor union practices limit

[8] West's book was accessed electronically and therefore page numbers are not easily identifiable.

the ability of the women workers to bargain for Fair Trade benefits from the plantation administration. Thus women in the plantation neither have a say in the ways in which the Fair-Trade premium (that the plantation receives each year) should be used nor do they have any clear idea of what Fair Trade entails (its history and benefits)" (Sen 2007).

This one example can be laminated over all the promotional marketing material that Americans are inundated with, even just as they stand in line at Whole Foods. People in the Global South become pawns in marketing ploys to convince people to buy Fair Trade, or donate to their cause, thus fueling the "cultural capitalist" market that has been constructed, and redeeming the unknowing consumer of her materialistic and humanistic guilt simultaneously.

It is the existence of these paradoxes that motivated the coffee industry to seek and build new models of trade within a commodity chain that has continually been reinvented across its history, yet always estranges and puts farmers in compromising situations.

Chapter three

Specialty Coffee, Direct Trade and the Third Wave

Specialty coffee is a term that encompasses any coffee grown at high elevation (above 4000 feet, up to 6000 feet), exhibiting unique flavor characteristics, that is judged on a hundred point scale at an 80 or above during cupping. Commercial coffee and Fair Trade coffee can be specialty coffee, but it is more often than not traded at higher prices than commercial-grade or non-specialty coffees. An institution based in California called the Specialty Coffee Association of America currently sets the standards and criteria for specialty grade and it is through this that many coffees in American cafes are judged and compared. They have partner institutions in Brazil, Guatemala, Taiwan, New Zealand and more.

Within the framework of post-industrial coffee consumption there have been three waves. First wave would be the NesCafe and instant coffees of the post-war era, out of which homebrew tinned coffee like Folger's was borne. In the 1960s, a group of young coffee professionals rejected this model and founded Peet's Coffee and Starbucks Coffee, respectively. These two cafes, which would go on to set the bar for other cafes worldwide, effectively kickstarted the second wave of coffee consumption. Second wave mirrored the mass produced consumer culture of the immediacy of the 90s. As a propellant for corporate America, second wave installed itself on every street corner to supplement the on-the-go new flock of business professionals. In true American fast food fascination, these cafes sold 500 calorie frappuccinos and cheesy breakfast sandwiches, promising swift transactions and drive-through service.

In the late 1990s, a new wave now known as third wave began emerging. The idea was to slow coffee down, and take it back to its roots as a social delicacy. Third wave is characterized by craftsmanship in preparation of coffee, quality over quantity, specialty grade only, sourcing from micro lots, and an emphasis on seed to cup supply chain dynamics. In 2009, Pulitzer Prize winning food critic Jonathon Gold of *LA Weekly* wrote, "We are now in the third wave of coffee connoisseurship, where beans are sourced from farms instead of countries, roasting is about bringing out rather than incinerating the unique characteristics of each bean, and the flavor is clean and hard and pure."[9] The third wave "big three" are notably Stumptown, based in Portland, Intelligentsia, based in Chicago, and Counter Culture of North Carolina. While those companies have established a name and a brand for themselves,

---

[9] http://www.laweekly.com/restaurants/la-mill-the-latest-buzz-2152451

cafes have been sprouting up exponentially since the early 2000s, ballooning to innumerable third wave shops boasting natural processed Guatemalan bourbons on La Marzocco espresso machines and pourovers of exclusive micro lot geshas for ten dollars a cup.

Within this framework, many third wave coffee shops select, source and roast all of their own coffee. "Green buyers" act as representatives, travelling to origin and selecting coffees as green beans, often freshly harvested, establishing professional relationships directly with farmers or with liaisons along the supply chain, either millers or exporters. This practice is known as "direct trade" and differs from commercial and fair trade in many ways that I will elucidate through ethnography.

Verve Coffee Roasters

Verve Coffee Roasters is a company based out of Santa Cruz that was opened in 2007 by Colby Barr and Ryan O'Donovan. Their idea to open a coffee shop was not unique. Since the first coffee shop had opened in Florence in 1548, possibly millions of coffee shops had come and gone. But what was different about Colby and Ryan was that they decided to join the movement called third wave, predicated upon specialty grade coffee, artisanal bar skills, and a "direct trade" relationship with farmers.

According to Colby[10], Verve got people's attention because they were early-adopters of third wave. Verve opened within the first year or two of third wave implementation. At that time, when a new third wave store opened, every person interested in specialty coffee heard about it. The market was unsaturated and unadul-

terated. Verve was on the short list of roasters that mattered. "We built a beautiful store, serving the best coffee, great roasting—Ryan is a great roaster—and we were obsessed with customer service," Colby said. One of the first wholesale accounts that catapulted Verve to national prominence was Café Grumpy in NY. A customer had brought them a bag of an Ethiopian coffee called Konga that blew them away. They called Verve and Colby answered the phone in between lattes and cappuccinos. Café Grumpy ordered 300 lbs. right

[10] Image: Left, Colby; Right, Ryan O'Donovan, pictured in Roastery for Kinfolk Magazine in 2013

then and there and Verve was one of their primary roasters for years. Today, Verve has had accounts in several countries, including Singapore, Japan, Great Britain, Philippines, and in Canada, Quebec, Montreal, totaling up to 350 accounts, including major Silicon Valley tech companies like Facebook, Yahoo, and DropBox.

Colby was raised listening to the Beatles and the Beach Boys on a Walkman as he harvested his father Ken's award-winning Blazing Star pears in Clearlake, California. He grew up as witness to the intricacies of agriculture and its supply chain. Along with the orchards, the Barrs had a packing facility on their farm. Ken had been a member of a co-op and after gaining success packing 500,000/36 lb. boxes per year, he came back and purchased the co-op. They also had a vineyard and Ken had gone to UC Davis for viticulture, marrying into pears. Ken wanted Colby to go to UC Davis and be a fellow Aggie like he was, but Colby wanted to choose a different school and a different path. He chose CSU Chico and received his degree in Environmental Studies and GIS, in between serving as jazz keyboardist for several bands and having near-death adventures, as most college students do. For a brief while he worked as a GIS mapping specialist, and was a contributor for the mapping of the catastrophic 2003 San Diego fire.

Just a year after purchasing The Naked Lounge, a coffee shop in Chico, California, he decided to apply his wisdom to the world of third wave coffee. He contacted college friend Ryan O'Donovan and together they launched Verve. Beginning in the popular surf neighborhood of Pleasure Point where Santa Cruz meets Capitola, Verve became lauded as a great café for strollers and beach cruisers, with families and local surfers rubbing elbows with out-of-towner coffee aficionados who flocked to the tiny 1000 sq. ft. store on 41st avenue for "spro" (slang for espresso) and to watch latte art being adorned on steamed milk beverages. Ryan roasted each batch of coffee by hand in the small 590 square foot building next door to the café, and had a large glass window installed next to the roaster to allow him to peer into the café to see if Colby needed help with the long line of customers.

Word spread and the line started getting longer as the world of specialty coffee started paying attention. Soon, Verve employed talented baristas like Chris Baca and Jared Truby who would go on to win Barista Competitions under Verve's flag.

In 2011 the demand for online wholesale coffee had exceeded the capacity of the 100 sq. ft. roastery space, Ryan and Colby invested in a 7,000 sq. ft. roastery, office space and half-outdoor café in the Seabright neighborhood in midtown Santa Cruz. From humble beginnings, soon the roastery was churning out 10,000 lbs. of roasted bean a week. Not far behind the Seabright space was the flagship store on Pacific Avenue, which opened in November of 2011 and is revered for its architectural innovation and ingenuity. Verve had hit the ground running at the perfect time for the market. Colby had originally intended to commute from Chico but when the momentum was at its peak, he moved to Santa Cruz permanently with the realization that what he had created had taken on a life of its own.

In addition to hosting and participating in several barista competitions and attracting ambitious young people, Verve cultivated a local culture that facilitated its easygoing vibe, all the while churning out expert and superlative coffee. Colby travels to each farm himself, meeting the producer and their family, getting to know the lay of the land and the types of terrain where specialty high-grown coffee thrives. After hours of cupping and deciphering, he decides which coffees to source, mill, and ship back to home base in Santa Cruz. Colby has served as green buyer since the beginning, and he has since brought on Jesse Crouse as a green buyer and flavor profile developer for Verve. He and Jesse split the travel responsibilities, travelling about a third of the year, scouting coffees in the heartland of Ethiopia, Kenya, Burundi, Rwanda, sometimes

Sumatra, and most frequently in Colombia, Guatemala, El Salvador, Costa Rica, Panama, and Honduras.

Verve has recently begun a large expansion. In 2013, CEO Chris Jordan was brought on the team with the goal to broaden Verve's horizons. In 2015, the first location outside of Santa Cruz was opened in Downtown Los Angeles. More cafes are in the works. The aim is that Verve's model to build a foundational business relationship with farmers can also grow within the same proportions as Verve's growth. With more revenue comes more opportunity to offer farmers premiums for their specialty coffees. In addition, the success of Verve afforded me a trip to experience origin and critically evaluate the conditions of the exchange relationship from an anthropological point of view.

CHAPTER FOUR
HONDURAS

Located in the heart of Central America, Honduras is a country slightly larger than the size of Tennessee, and home to eight million people, half of whom live rurally and in abject poverty.[11] Honduras is known globally for being the second poorest country in Central America, and for having the world's highest murder rate per capita.[12] It has a short pacific coastline and a large Caribbean coastline. The capital and most populous city is Tegucigalpa. Ninety percent of the population is mestizo, or a mix of European and Amerindian descent as a result of 300 years of Spanish colonialism. The remainder of the population is divided amongst indigenous peoples, white, and black, including the black and indigenous group called Garifuna who have been native to Honduras since the 1500s.

---

[11]ruralpovertyportal.org/country/statistics/tags/honduras

[12] CIA World factsheet||www.cia.gov/library/publications/the-world-factbook/geos/ho.html

The high murder rate can be attributed to extreme poverty, lack of infrastructure and gang violence.

Like most of Central America, the transnational connection with America is ubiquitous, whether it be in the logos that adorn the cultural landscape, the t-shirts that say "GAP" or "Levi's," or the fact that remittances from immigrant Hondurans working in America is one of the country's main source of income. UCSC anthropology professor Mark Anderson's field work has focused on the Garifuna of Honduras and that group's association with what Anderson labels "Black America." He uses fashion as a catalyst for a conversation of transnational identities that transcend superficial symbols we wear and form a deeper meaning of power dynamics. "My account here is one of how the consumption of styles culled from Black America by Garifuna men in Honduras involves mimetic practices that tap into the figure of a similar other across the social and symbolic chasm separating the North and the South" (Anderson 2009:178). Anderson and I both see distillations and distance between these two places, united by and divided by the colonial inequities of the past, perpetrated by the North onto the South.

Using the Global Northern markers of the GDP and HDI, Honduras has a gross domestic product of 18.55 billion, and a GDP per capita of 2,290. The country that purchases most of Honduras's coffee, the United States, has a gross domestic product of over 16 trillion and a GDP per capita of 53,000, comparatively. Honduras is ranked as the 120th country out of 187 on the Human Development Index, which is "a summary measure for assessing long-term progress in three basic dimensions of human development: a long and healthy life, access to knowledge and a decent standard of living.[13]" America is ranked 5th.

Honduras' political history is erratic. Though it managed to come away as the only unscathed country during the civil wars each Central American country experienced in the 1980s, Honduras has had a revolving door of leaders, ousted presidents, military dictatorships, and a huge gang presence that has swelled to overwhelm the majority of Honduran citizens, especially in the capital city of Tegucigalpa. The gang presence is tied to the transnational connections that Anderson speaks of, with movement of people, drugs, and crime flowing between the borders.

Judging by these facts and number alone, the playing field is far from level. Yet, the global coffee market operates under conditions where those from the Global North extract resources from the Global South. It is a business transaction that offers the

---

[13] http://hdr.undp.org

promise of a stable living for producers, or in the case of direct trade, the glimmer of a more comfortable wage, yet carries with it the extreme risk of losing it all.

The Benitez family

Chapter Five
Ethnography
In the field: Santa Barbara, Honduras

When Colby and I flew to Honduras in May of 2014, we first stopped in Guatemala where we had an unexpected layover for five hours. We spent it in the executive lounge, sipping cokes and talking about music, and I looked down on the sidewalk below where people were arriving and departing, shuffling luggage and honking horns. Occasionally announcements or advertisements would sound over the intercom, entirely in Spanish.

The flight from Guatemala to San Pedro Sula was less than an hour long, and when we landed in the country's second largest city, I felt a wall of tropical air hit me. It was around four PM and our delay had gotten us there 18 hours after leaving America. Shops selling bags of candies and pork rinds were awaiting us at the terminal, the female shopkeepers perched on stools with sweat beads on their foreheads and shoulders slumped forward in exhaustion and boredom. My eyes were wide open, scanning over the faces and buildings and I wasn't tired from the day's journey. Colby was on the phone with Benjamin Paz, the son of the owner of Beneficio San Vicente who would be our liaison for the long weekend. We walked out the doors of the airport and Benjamin was awaiting us. Benjamin is 28, handsome with short black hair, an oval face, and is always wearing Verve shirts and jeans. He speaks Spanish and English fluently, and received a degree in Business Administration. “I got that just in order to fill my Dad's requirement to have a title, because I didn't like school,” he wrote to me in an email.

He greeted us and then quickly escorted us to his black early-2000s pick-up truck. He generously took our bags and hoisted them into the bed of his truck, all the while assuring Colby that he hadn’t minded waiting, and that he’d killed time by visiting friends and eating lunch in San Pedro Sula. Benjamin and Colby sat in front and I huddled in the back amidst power cables and boxes. The parking lot for the airport was feet away from the terminal, and the whole building was the same size as a small shopping mall. Two left turns and we were out on a main highway. Soon the urban sprawl and decay of San Pedro Sula was unfolding outside the window.

I stayed silent as Benjamin and Colby caught up. They spoke of mutual friends, memories, the United States Barista Competition, Benjamin’s recent visit to the states and other green buyers Benjamin had served as liaison. Benjamin’s father Fidel owns the beneficio, or mill, that processes the majority of the coffee produced in the Santa Barbara region. His job, in addition to working at the mill, doing cuppings and quality control, is to host and facilitate visiting green buyers like Colby from Verve, Ryan from Madcap, Darrin from Stumptown, Geoff from Intelligentsia, Stephen Vick from Blue Bottle, Steve Ford from Ritual, Matt from Coava, (and many more) so that they can see, taste and experience the coffee and meet the producers. Benjamin brokers the sales and send coffee processed at the mill to the exporters where it'll eventually be shipped to the importer, then make it back into the hands of either a third party or in house roaster, which in Verve's case is one operation.

I scanned the countryside as it became cityscape. Roads lined with discarded paper, glass and plastic wrappers and bottles. Haphazard lean-tos made of defunct Coca-Cola billboards, lonely dogs roaming solo. People standing in aimless clusters, watching the cars zoom by. Roadside fruit sands boasting bananas and Pepsi, *pupusas* and mangoes. Two women and a teenage boy in a pink shirt sharing a red umbrella to shade themselves from the sun, still hot as it started to set. Tin roofs turned orange with rust. Abandoned industrial projects left to crumble in cement graveyards. Palm trees and power cords. Three men in hats carrying plastic bags of fruit, sitting casually in the middle of the divided highway. Vans converted into public transportation with eighties style painted logos. A Kia car dealership that had no cars for sale, decrepit and lonely. At a stoplight a woman sat with papayas and citrus to sell, but she had given up, resorting to sitting languorously behind her sign. A truck idled next to us carrying twenty-five head of cattle crammed behind a slotted metal enclosure. A woman selling clothes and garments from a plastic box roamed the aisles of cars. A man in a yellow shirt waved to cars, a full three-gallon jug of water perched on his shoulder. We came across a marketplace with wooden stalls offering jewelry and assorted t-shirts with American brands and English words scrawled across the front. Nike, Adidas. A Wendy's restaurant sign reigned high in the sky above the signs for local huts and shops, and parked out front were a line of red rickshaw-style taxis.

I didn't know where we were going or what to expect, but our drive from the airport ended up lasting two hours. The road looped through rural grasslands and started sloping upward as we approached Peña Blanca, the village at the base of the mountain. Benjamin pulled off the road to what looked like a practice soccer field. A dark empty building next to it was where we would eat. It seemed like no one was around, yet Benjamin transferred our suitcases into the cab of the truck to make sure no one stole anything. We ate outside as the sky grew dimmer in twilight. My feet, exposed in sandals, became dinner for about a dozen mosquitoes.

We drove further into the village after dinner and pulled up in front of what looked like someone's house—our hotel for the night. Nearby, nightlife was just revving up. A parked food truck had a line of hungry revelers queued up around plastic tables. Mariachi music played in the distance. Trucks drove by with 20 or so standing passengers in their truck beds. Colby made sure we all had bottles of water before Benjamin left, the potential of water-borne disease was too great to risk it, even for brushing teeth. Benjamin said he'd pick us up bright and early the next morning and left Colby and me to share cheap cervesas and talk about Verve's history and future on the front lawn of the hotel as more truckloads of people drove by, laughing and shouting.

From Seed to Cup

Benefició San Vicente sits on an industrial road down a street from the center of Peña Blanca, where we'd spend humid gray mornings eating tropical fruit and pupusas at a food shack called El Riñcon del Sabor. Benjamin owned a café two shops down from our breakfast spot, and there in the air-conditioned lobby that resembled any café in my hometown, he had his baristas prepare espressos and pour-overs for us.

Out in front of the mill are large drying patios and loading docks. Inside, huge sorting machines tower over in rows, shelling parchment and sifting for density. From seed to cup, the processing of coffee consists of five steps, generally. There are four main types of coffee processing, 1) wet, 2) dry or natural, 3) pulped natural or honey processed, and 4) semi-washed. First, ripe red cherries are picked by hand from the shrubs, which each generate about 2000 useable cherries. From there, the cherries are sorted by density. Sometimes this is done by hand and sight, other times it involves floating them in sorting beds filled with water. The denser cherries sink and the lighter ones are scooped off the surface. The denser the cherry, the more desirable the bean within. They way the skin is removed determines which one of the four processes is being utilized. During the washed process, after sorting, the cherries are mechanically pulped to separate the fruit of the cherry from the coffee beans inside. Some farms have pulping stations on site. After pulping, the beans are still coated in a slick membrane called the mucilage. Then, the beans are soaked in water and fermented until it naturally peels off. After this stage, the beans are in what is known as the "parchment" stage because the only layer left is a very fine layer of skin that won't be milled off until it is fully dried and sent to a place like Beneficio San Vicente to complete the process.

Dry processed coffees differ from washed in that the cherry is not removed but rather is left on the cherries to dry in the sun on hot patios, usually in Ethiopia and Brazil where distinct dry seasons have made this method part of traditional coffee production. During the drying process, compounds from the fruit diffuse through the parchment and into the seed, enriching it with sugars and endowing the bean with a sweetness that will come across as heavy, fragrant fruitiness when brewed. After drying, the mucilage is mechanically hulled and only parchment remains to be sorted for defects, usually by hand.

Similar to the dry process is the honey process, during which beans are processed similar to washed processed beans, but the mucilage is left intact in varying degrees which determine the stage of "honey." For example, beans with only minimal mucilage are called white honey, ranging in levels through yellow and red all the way up to black honey, where the entire mucilage is left on. Drying in parchment on patios or in covered drying screens, the beans end up being much sweeter than washed coffees, with a subdued acidity and clarity.

Semi-washed is a lesser-used process that is utilized in Indonesia where beans are washed and pulped but the beans are left in their mucilage and sealed in plastic bags to begin the demucilage process during transit to the mill. This process can work well, or it can leave the coffee with an astringent sourness that is characteristic of some Sumatran coffees.

At Beneficio San Vicente, beans arrive in the parchment stage and are sample cupped to examine quality and taste. When approved for sale they are milled and sent to the exporter. Up a flight of stairs and through a glass door that warns "No Eating! No Drinking!" is the lab. The lab is where all the cupping takes place, which is why no other goods or beverages can be present (so as to not contaminate the flavor of the coffee in question). During cupping, coffees are ground, brewed, slurped and evaluated, blindly. It's critical that cuppings be conducted blind so that no bias can sway grading. Cup of Excellence cuppings are all performed blind, and Colby swears by it. In the green buyers issue of The Specialty Coffee Chronicle, Colby was interviewed as saying, "Always, always, always cup blind. Don't drink your own Kool-Aid. I also like to re-cup a few times (again, blind) to prove to myself that I believe what I believe. This is especially helpful when narrowing selections at origin...Cupping blind is the answer"[14]. People participating in cuppings should remain silent and wear poker faces, keeping emotions and scribbled notes private to discourage opinions. Coffees receive a grade on a 100-point scale. Specialty grade is 80 and above, but Colby usually doesn't buy below 86. The highest score he's ever given for a coffee sold at Verve was a 92 for the award-winning Elida Estate Green-Tip Gesha from Boquette, Panama. As a judge at CoE he once gave a 94 to a Guatemalan Pacamara called El Injerto.

If there were the equivalent of sommeliers for coffee, Colby would be one of them. His pallet is highly sensitive to even the slightest hint of a certain flavor. Granted, all taste is subjective, but Colby has been at it for so long that he can identify the gamut of coffee-wheel flavors and descriptors (vegetal, mahogany, white grape, tobacco, honeydew, structured, balanced, complex, heavy, astringent, et al) and he has code words for a lot of them. One of my triumphant moments was grading two of the coffees the same grade as Colby. That afternoon, we cupped two times, about fifteen coffees each. We were in lab, circling the table—slurping, spitting, scribbling—for about three hours. It was there that I was first

[14] The Specialty Coffee Chronicle, a Publication of the Specialty Coffee Association of America, 2014 issue no. 2

introduced to Arturo Paz, Benjamin's cousin, and owner of one of the highest farms on the mountain, La Colmena. His coffee had been offered in 2013 as a white label reserve coffee, which Verve saves for exclusive premieres, small lots, and coffees that are deemed more unique than others. Arturo, Benjamin and Colby all aspirate their coffee fully, rigorously, stridently. I sound like someone with strep throat limply tilting broth into her mouth. But still, flavors appear to me, some better than others.

Highlights from our second cupping included an 86 for La Fortuna, a farm owned by the Madrid family. I wrote "apple, complex" and Colby said, "tropical, lasting, limón, miel del blanco (white honey)" it was everyone's favorite on the table. Another coffee that I rated at an 86 had notes of raspberry and cranberry. It belonged to Juan Benitez, a farmer with whom Colby had never worked. We decided to go pay him a visit. We grabbed lunch and then headed up the rugged crags of montaña Santa Barbara.

Farmlevel

I perched in the middle backseat of a truck with Colby and one other man, hanging on to the side of the passenger seat in front of me and Benjamin's seat to keep steady as the cab bucked and swished, careening over hills and down slopes. My only seatbelt were the two knees on either side of me, equally tensed and stressed as we all tried to keep ourselves upright under the pressure of surmounting the steep mountain road. It was a distance of probably only 10 miles or so, but it took well over an hour to get there due to the harrowing rocky conditions of the road. Benjamin had one hand on the clutch and one on the wheel, chatting casually with his associate in the front seat and driving the road he knew so well. Colby pointed out both natural and cultivated coffee plants as they raced past our window. Using what we fondly called "CIS" (Colby Information Systems, because of his GIS background and insane geographical memory) he could point out the window and tell stories of the year before: who owns what farm, which green buyers buy from which farms.

It was on this late afternoon trip that I first bore witness to the devastation of roya, the airborne fungus that had devastated nearly 25% of Central America's coffee production (ICO.org). Virtually every farmer was at risk, and everyone had to be taking precautions against the ailment—adding nutrition to the soil, obsessively trimming and weeding, using calcium and other vitamins—or else pay the price with their plants' lives. It takes five years for a plant to mature, but some farmers had to sacrifice by hacking the plant altogether and starting over when the roya was beyond reproach. "See the red dots on the leaves," Colby said, pointing as we slowly rolled past a farm. Half of it had been clear cut, the farmer resorting to take a loss, trim and start letting the plants mature again in the hopes of fighting off the roya. To maximize resources and make a silver lining out of such a tremendous disadvantage, many farmers had kept the trimmed stalks of their coffee plants and reused them, turning them into fences and firewood. We drove past bundles and bundles of tightly bunched, precision-cut stalks ready to be repurposed, a grim coffee graveyard. In this issue is reflected the risk that comes along with farming, and the lives that are at stake, hoping that they'll still be able to make ends meet when their entire crop is wiped out. Who can be accountable in this and how can farmers gain a sense of security in such an uncertain market?

Finally we pulled off and into a long driveway that lead to red shack and a drying bed, owned by a man named Natividad. This was the end of the line for the truck; we'd have to hike from there. Natividad and his wife stood around the shack and dryer, and Benjamin consulted with them in Spanish. Children in bare feet and dirty t-shirts and shorts ran around, partially curious of us newcomers. Inside the plastic sheet of the dryer, the air was much warmer. Raised beds with little white coffee beans lined the arced structure, about fifteen feet long. We ran our hands in the beans, spreading them out, scooping them up and inhaling deeply. To me, it smelled like baker's chocolate, slightly bitter, dry, sweet. Back outside, we began the trek up the muddy mountainside, slipping and tripping our way over boulders and puddles. Above, at another landing about ten minutes' walk from Natividad's drying beds, stood Juan Benitez's house. It was a cement-floored shack with red tin walls, dark inside. His wife and twelve children loitered around outside, happy to receive us. One boy about nine was very curious and he followed us up and down the mountain.

The farm was sloped severely, with a garden and bushes of flowers suddenly making way to rows and rows of coffee spanning up the mountainside. Juan Benitez had one horse that was wandering around with the little boy, almost like a dog. I struggled through Spanish phrases and pointed at the horse saying, "*Caballo? Caballo, verdad*?" The little boy just smiled with gapped teeth, a mischievous and interested countenance. Don Juan appeared, a blue denim button up on, one panel tucked in, one panel left out, dirt patches covering it, a straw hat, rugged jeans, boots. In his weathered hands he held a pick axe-sized scythe that he busied himself with, hacking at weeds. He seemed disinterested in us, trying to finish his work. He smiled, most of his teeth missing, and shook our hands, but then went back to work hacking. The air was cold and the chorus of clandestine tropical birds rang throughout, soaring over the hill and down toward Lago de Yojoa, an oval of tourmaline below.

This was my first time standing amongst actual coffee plants. Colby continuously picked me handfuls of cherries. Red, orange, yellow, each with distinct flavors of fruits like banana, papaya. Colby was so excited about the flavors of the cherries, which is usually an indicator of complex roasted coffee. As Juan Benitez hacked and tended to his farm, Colby asked him little questions through Benjamin but we mostly trudged through the bushes alone.

Eventually, we got him to put down his scythe and stand still for an interview. He spoke in Spanish and Benjamin was our intermediary. He told us he was 54 years old and had been farming coffee for ten years. "It's the only thing that you can really see that gives you advancement, I have worked with corn and beans, I have done things, but in coffee it really moves you forward, motivation," he said. It was obvious he was a hard worker, and he attributed his farm's success to weeding and fertilizer.

When asked how specialty coffee has changed his life, the reaction was sudden and emphatic.

> JUAN BENITEZ: If it wasn't for specialty coffee, I'd be wounded...with this it provides, the cost is high, even then I still have money problems, but it helps me.
> KATIE SLOCUM: How was it back then?
> JUAN: Before I had trouble selling my coffee, I put it in a big box and sold it somewhere, but now it's different. With the late harvest, the warehouses closed, and I'd have to keep it here and sell it green later for cheaper.

Colby added that, while most conventional coffee buyers shy away from late harvest, he is a seeker of late-harvest coffees like Juan's that might be more special due to their peak growing and harvesting time.

> KATIE: Does he feel like specialty coffee is helping him gain access to more resources?
> JUAN: *Sí, sí.*
> BENJAMIN PAZ: That's a solid yes. The market is good right now. He's getting twice as much for his coffee, because of you guys.
> COLBY BARR: I want to tell him that we love his coffee and that's why we come here, to form a long-term relationship and that want to be able to develop this quality coffee program together, as we grow, he grows, we grow together.

JUAN: Hearing that, I'm going to continue working, and I'm not going to miss the opportunity of having someone who has interest. I'm going to be happy getting those prices.
COLBY: It's a deal!

Verve ultimately purchased 1064 pounds of Juan Benitez's coffee at $4/lb.

THE RELATIONSHIP AND ITS LIMITATIONS

Colby bases all his interactions with producers on the premise of a relationship. But what does that mean for both parties? In Colby's words, he says:

> I would say it means that we want to create a connection where there is an expectation that we will act as a client of theirs in years to come and they as a supplier, so long as we meet each other's requirements and expectations. Those usually revolve around price, quantity, and quality.
> In addition to these business basics, we want to create trust and goodwill between each other so that we can talk openly to each other about how it's going. The old days, every link in the supply chain had to fight each other. We want to create win/win wherever possible, not win/whatever.
> (email interview).

The next day on our way up the hill to visit more farms and producers, the truck was forced to stop at a section of the road that had been torn up with a bulldozer. We had to hike about an hour up the mountain to get to Rodrigo Erazo's farm. La Mina is one of the highest farms on the mountain, at 1800 meters or 5905 feet. Specialty coffee is interested in the range of 4000-6000 foot range, but the higher the better. Elevation impacts the coffee by making it denser, the beans harder and more flavor-packed. The environmental conditions that occur at that high of an elevation slow the maturation process and lead to the late harvest that Juan Benitez mentioned. The hike to his farm took about an hour and a half by foot, and afforded us some time to stare down the mountainside at the lilting valleys and forests blanketing the region. We reached his farm by midday and paused to drink some bottled water near his washing station. There were vibrant flowers lining the pathway up to his plants, his cement processing station, and little else. More importantly, Rodrigo was nowhere to be seen. I figured it was just a lapse of communication but once we saw the state of his farm, I started wondering if he was intentionally avoiding us.

The plants were grayish brown, withered and twisted, covered in red roya patches. The aisles were overgrown like wild thistles and not navigable by foot. We stood at the farm's edge, staring out over the destruction. Colby was noticeably disappointed and I was, too. The question became what to do? Verve's responsibility to its customers is to deliver the best possible coffee, yet its responsibility to its producers is to sustain a relationship based on higher than market value prices for its coffee. The conundrum was how to proceed when coffee isn't sellable.

As we trekked back down the hill, Colby expressed the ethical dilemma he was having in regards to purchasing La Mina in the state it was in.

> COLBY: One of our all-stars last year, La Mina, this year is almost a no-go, because...of the roya, but is it because of the roya or is it because of farm management? Which is what we were talking about earlier. Which is basically the paradox of what do you do, Verve farmlevel direct trade, what does it even mean? But I guess... what would we do with farmers in this situation when the coffee doesn't show up good? So, using the example of Rodrigo Erazo of La Mina, the question is what do we do? We're cupping it, it's not tasting good at all, like an 85. I mean, it's tasting okay, the coffee could sell and be specialty grade coffee, but it's not boutique, it's definitely not what it was last year, it's not stellar, but it's not boutique, it doesn't even really qualify for any level of verve buying, for even Buena Vista or whatever. So

what do we do, right? The problem is that, as we saw on his farm, it's just hammered.

KATIE: What did it look like?

COLBY: The trees? Well, they're scraggly, missing a lot of leaves, they look very weak, you can tell it's been hit with roya really hard, but in addition to being hit with roya really hard—which is the loss of leaves which makes them look spindly—you can also see all the old roya marks on the leaves, that's littered throughout the farm, but it's also that the weakness that you see is because of a lack of a focused nutrition program, fertilizer. Which, when we talked to Juan Benitez and asked him what does he do to combat rust, he straight up said, "fertilize." 'Cause, you know, that's one thing you can do besides applying a fungicide, is actually just try to make the plant as healthy as possible and as strong as possible to actually fight the roya itself. And I think what we were seeing up there, underneath the trees, the leaves were kind of yellowing, it's just not, the nutrient program is not being delivered. So then, the question is what do we do, right?

K: Because we want to sustain that relationship.

C: Yeah, we want to sustain the relationship, and Verve is quote unquote all about the relationships, but I think the most important thing to remember when we talk about the farmlevel program, is that we lead by quality. You know, we lead by quality, so like, Brit [McCorquodale, former marketing advisor] made this quote, which I think is actually incredible, it's "cupping blind with open eyes" which is to say, we cup blind, but it's not that we don't care or don't want to have any connection to the coffee, we also wanna have a total connection to the coffee, that's why we're still walking on this hill still for hour number what, two or three? To get to this farm, that we're probably not gonna be able to buy, just to see it firsthand, and try to figure out the plan.

Because, we can't buy this coffee because if we're in our café, and we put up La Mina this year and people come in and it says "now brewing La Mina" and they buy it and they drink it and everyone's like, "God, this coffee doesn't taste very good; Verve's coffee isn't tasting very good," and it says La Mina* with an asterisk and we say, "Oh the asterisk means the coffee isn't very good this year, but you know, we bought it because we need to, like, support the producer, even though he could have done a nutrient program and done some things to help, but he didn't because he's old school."

As Benjamin said, he's [Rodrigo] kind of old school and set in his ways, but that's not an excuse to have that, you know, farming practices that are not producing good coffee and we say, "well, you know it's cool, just buy it anyway, you need to support the farmers because you're in the supply chain, and then like next year maybe it'll be better." People would just not buy our coffee, or like, stop coming to Verve.

> Even though people totally want to reward us for farmlevel and buying direct, and having sustainable buying practices, they come to our stores because we have amazing coffee and amazing service. And, we are in a supply chain, fortunately I think, we are in a supply chain built on quality, that gets to reward farmers for quality, and build a channel for them to take a ton of pride and put their work in, and see that reward come of their hard work by developing quality and then we pay premium for that quality. That doesn't exist for a lot of farmers. So, to have a farmer that has one of the best addresses in Honduras, at over 1700 meters, 1750 meters, that has roya and the trees aren't healthy, and they're spindly and they haven't been pruned or rejuvenated, and they're not being fertilized, are we supposed to just buy that coffee anyway because we bought it last year?
>
> (recorded voice transcript).

Verve's hesitance to buy "subpar" coffee and Rodrigo Erazo's inability to comply to the demands of commodity farming reflect a dynamic of risk that Megan Moodie discusses in her article, "Microfinance and the Gender of Risk." Moodie asserts that when those in a position of power—whether that be in an economic sense as in this case—withdraw support from someone with less power, the risk is always greater on the bottom. Farmers everywhere hope that the conditions of their farm stay regulated enough to yield a sufficient crop, but run the risk that it won't, as in the case of La Mina.

In subsequent cuppings, La Mina began to grade higher, and Verve was able to offer Erazo an average of $3.15/lbs for 760 total pounds of his early and late harvest combined, $3.75 for late harvest and $2.75 for early harvest. The only difference was it would be blended into dark roast coffees to disguise any taste deficiencies, as opposed to being featured as a single origin offering. This particular case was a close call, but what happens when the coffee can't be purchased at all?

To get to the bottom of this issue, I turned to two knowledgeable sources within the upper management of Verve. Chris Jordan has been the CEO of Verve for two years. He started his career in coffee the way I did, as an entry-level Starbucks partner. Within ten years, he had ascended up through store manager to the green coffee program and global development, taking the company international and integrating programs like Fair Trade and Starbucks Farmer Support Centers. Before coming to Verve, he worked for two Africa-based companies. Dorman's, which is a coffee roaster and wholesaler based out of Kenya focused on corporate social responsibility, and Technoserve, a nonprofit funded by the Bill and Melinda Gates Foundation to implement agronomic and sustainability programs to support thousands of Ethiopian farmers. I spoke with him about mitigating farmer risk and business's responsibility to producers in impoverished areas. "Rejection due to quality happens universally," he lamented. "The farmer could either make corrections or sell to someone else who may not offer as much money, but it can still be sold commercially." (phone interview).

I asked him if he'd hypothetically be willing to implement a secure program wherein farmers with whom Verve enter into a relationship are compensated regardless of crop catastrophes. Immediately he said, "Of course," and offered potential solutions, such as long-term advance contracts where producers could receive funding via Verve and use it to nurse a potentially damaged farm back to health, should a catastrophe occur, so that Verve could invest in future crops.

Matt Broscio is Verve's most recently hired member, who also worked at Technoserve, and has been a social responsibility intern for such companies as Peet's Coffee. He has been brought onto Verve to focus on community and social impact, which includes maintaining records of premiums given to farmers to ensure the green buying program is as fair and efficient as possible, while also keeping business objectives in mind. He echoed Jordan's sentiments when he agreed that the current model at Verve is not sufficient in making farmers feel secure. He envisions a future where farmers are awarded a type of insurance for their crops and where Verve backs farmers up in case of emergency. He agrees that there must be failsafes to mitigate risk but he suggests the solution is in finding the balance between corporate and individual responsibility. "I think that to some extent there is a level of responsibility that the farmers have to take on, and a certain extent of responsibility that Verve has to take on, and I don't know if anyone in specialty coffee has figured out what that balance is. We have to be engaging in a responsible way with farmers, but still maintaining business objectives," he said (phone interview). For his first project working with Verve, he's taking on outlining that plan and figuring out the best way to give farmers confidence and security, while upholding Verve's business objectives.

Subsequent Farm Visits in Santa Barbara

After visiting Rodrigo Erazo's farm, La Mina, we trekked back down the hill to return to the truck, some miles down. On the road we encountered another of the mountain's producers, Danilo P.

Danilo was wearing nice Levi's, a white dress shirt with rolled up sleeves, and a red baseball had with "New York" embroidered on it in black thread. He had a trim black mustache and kind smile lines. Hoisted over his shoulder was a machete wrapped in newspaper, a reusable shopping bag hooked on to the end and he held the blade casually, his hands clasped and relaxed. He was happy to speak to us and knew Benjamin somewhat. Benjamin translated as Danilo explained to us that he had been working on a nursery of new coffee plants but had lost them due to frost. Meanwhile, he's been tending to his old farm, cleaning and pruning, and gathering resources to focus on a new farm filled with yellow and red catuai and pacas at around 1700 meters, a very high elevation farm. To finance his farm's needs he would pick wild blackberries in the forest and sell them, sometimes upwards of 100 pounds of blackberries.

He spoke in depth about combating roya, and the extensive pruning he had been required to do to rid his bourbon plants of the fungus. He had employed fungicides, calcium, copper sulfate and ashes, determining that calcium works better. Diligently, he would apply the calcium every fifteen days to combat the rust.

Colby and Benjamin inquired how specialty coffee had affected Danilo's life. He replied that he didn't see it as a business, but as help, to lift him out of what used to be poor conditions and low prices, as low as forty cents a pound.

BENJAMIN: Now he's getting 12 times more.
COLBY: Because you're up on the hill, disconnected from the marketplace. Back then.
BENJAMIN: And he says thank you, for all the help you guys putting in, and also pushing to help developing these relationships, and that's why he keeps working, and he's looking forward to getting better, and growing.
COLBY: Well I want to thank him for the coffee, the opportunity, and the relationship, and we're here for long-term, and if he keeps focusing on quality, we'll keep looking to support him the best we can, in this family. BENJAMIN: He says that he doesn't want to go backwards, and that he's always thinking ahead and preparing. Last year, he got six bags of parchment, and you got three bags of exportable, so this year it's going to be different, he's going to get an additional two bags, because he was able to work better, and he's motivating his kids to help him to continue working.
COLBY: *Mucho gusto.*
DANILO: *Igualmente!*

Verve ultimately purchased 608 pounds of Danilo's coffee at $2.75/lb.

Parting ways from Danilo, we continued down the rugged mountainside, over the trench that had forced us to abandon the truck earlier, the bulldozer now sitting vacant, inanimate, and drove back through the town of Peña Blanca to grab lunch and regroup. The next farm we were to visit belonged to Leonisio Castellon and was on a different slope of the mountain. Leonisio's farm was much lower down in elevation, sitting at 1340 meters or about 4440 feet. To get there, we drove through neighborhoods of pallid adobe stone houses, contrasted against the vibrant green of the grass and the grey sky of the late afternoon. Humid air rushed in through the truck's open windows and I watched as we passed by the blurred watercolors of houses and buildings. We slowed down and pulled off the side of the paved road. His farm was so low that we didn't have to climb back up the vertical mountain slope.

Leonisio's farm was impeccable, completely flat, plants with deep emerald leaves, crisp coffee cherries the color of strawberries in mid-June. To get to his rows of catuai, we walked past his drying bed, where about five people were crouched, sorting cherries by hand, and through his garden where he grew cover crops like squash, plantain and cabbage. Lining the plants like sentinels were large trees he had planted to loom over the coffee as a wind barrier. Within the rows were scattered taller trees planted to cast shade, because at this elevation there was no cloud cover relied on by farmers at higher elevations, and the unforgiving sun required intervention to protect the coffee.

Leonisio himself was tall, quiet and soft-spoken, wearing a purple polo shirt. He seemed a lot younger than the other farmers I'd met so far. He said he'd had that farm for eleven years. He answered our questions amidst the verdant shrubs, offering short, concise sentences almost in a timid manner. Leonisio said that for him, farming was a family matter, having passed down from his predecessors and continuing on with his wife and two children who helped him tend to the farm. When asked about roya and how he kept his farm so beautiful and healthy, he cited nutrition, fertilizer, diversification of crops, shade and ventilation as his ammunition against the fungus. As always, we asked him what he thought about specialty coffee and the difference it has made on his life. Our trusty translator Benjamin was there to interpret his answer.

> COLBY: What does he think about, since last year was his first year coming into specialty, how has that affected his life?
>
> LEONISIO: The first thing is that I can give my family a better way of living. Also, now I have enough resources to maintain and take care of the farm. Before, I didn't have enough resources to make

everything work this well. The main thing that I think all the farmers should be thinking of: Taking care of family, taking care of farms.

COLBY: It's a cycle. *Familia y finca.*

LEONISIO: Of course.

Verve bought more of Leonisio's coffee than of any of the other Honduran producers we visited on this trip: 2584 at $3.86/lb.

Before driving to the last farm of the day, we drove back through town and picked up the producer, our friend Franklin Madrid with whom we'd already spent some time deliberating around the cupping table. Franklin and his family own several farms in the El Sauce region of Santa Barbara and, after taking first place in 2008, have placed in the top fifteen of Cup of Excellence three times in the last three years. Of the Madrid family, Franklin's farm La Patepluma had placed the highest, ranked at 7th in 2014.

Franklin is sharp. Sharp dresser, sharp intellect, eager salesperson. His short black hair he always wears slicked back with gel, and he wears nice watches and always has a smile on his face. His farm La Patepluma lies between the farms of his brothers and father on a slope of the mountain which, on that particular afternoon just before the sunset, was circled by dense fog and sprinkled with large boulders of quartz. Looking down the farm to the horizon there are layers of shadowed mountains, the village seated in between peaks and curves of the surrounding foothills. He stood against this majestic background as he zealously answered our questions, his blue, white and red Ralph Lauren shirt clashing with the resplendent green. Pointing down and around his land, he identified his family's farms.

> FRANKLIN: This is the family farm. Every member of the family has their own lot. (Pointing) The finca Cristal belongs to my brother, Jose Estefan Madrid's, when we were coming up on this hill, another brother, Lenin, owns Flor del Cafe. To the right is the farm of my father, El Sauce. There are four brothers, we are the fourth generation of coffee producers, passed down through inheritance. Our whole life revolves around coffee.

Franklin admitted that, before the Madrid family realized their coffee was such high quality, they were selling it commercially, receiving one-third of what he is paid now for his coffee.

Verve purchased 1064 pounds of coffee from Franklin at $4/lb. In 2013 Verve purchased Franklin's first harvest on this farm, and in 2015 Verve also released a single origin coffee from Franklin's newest farm, La Fortuna. It was his first harvest, something that companies might resist because of the lower maturity level of the plants, but Verve supported it and it ended up being a sweetly complex coffee, bursting with similar melon and tropical flavors that I remember tasting on La Patepluma that day as we interviewed him.

After the interview concluded, the golden sun broke through the dense cloud cover, bathing the plants in a crystalline shower of amber rays. Colby, Franklin, Benjamin and I stood in the light, taking pictures and laughing with each other like old friends. Another time Colby had visited this area, he spent six hours playing soccer with these guys and some other family members. As the sun sank down behind Santa Barbara, I too felt like I was a part of something bigger, bridging cultural gaps and uniting under one plant that brings people from all walks of life together every day globally. Benjamin once wrote to me in an email,

> I can say I had to love coffee even if I didn't wanted to (it is great that I do). Coffee means a lot to me, My Dad and my Mom met when my grandfather went to pick coffee at my other grandfather's house. He was 20, she was 16. I was able to study, eat, play and meet my favorite friends because of coffee. I live it every single day, I touch it, brew it or do something with it everyday, it is life for me and my family. Just think, we met and we are doing all this because of coffee,

> you are talking to a Honduran who lives hundreds miles away from you just because of that drink, beautiful drink.

The following morning we had our last breakfast of delicious fresh papaya, mango and cantaloupe and final cupping at the mill before heading up to La Colmena with Arturo Paz, manager of the Beneficio San Vicente and Benjamin's cousin. Arturo is in his early thirties, with crew cut blonde hair and piercing blue eyes. Like Benjamin, he can speak English and conducted his entire interview with us in it, but it's a little less polished. His gorgeous farm, La Colmena, is the highest on its slope at 1700 meters, with nothing but the national forest above it. He grows red catuai, saying that it withstands the wind better than bourbon would. His farm is a difficult place to grow coffee because it is so cold, with the sun barely shining, and the intense winds.

Yet, Arturo's coffee is continually exceptional quality. In 2013 he placed 7th in the Cup of Excellence. That same year, Verve featured his coffee as a white label reserve, which is reserved for coffees that are deemed more unique, distinctive, or those that Verve has purchased a smaller quantity. He's been growing at that spot since 2008 and he says due to the conditions of his farm, he has only harvested twice. "It's difficult because you need to clean the farm very quickly, because the soil is very rich...and the plants grow very slow. I had to wait five years to make my first harvest. Nobody in two years you can harvest" Arturo said as we stood amidst his perfectly manicured rows of coffee. In between filming, he took out shears from his pocket, clearing old growth and letting his plants breathe.

> COLBY: How did you become involved in specialty coffee?
>
> ARTURO: Because I am the manager of the mill, the *beneficio*, quality control, definitely we start in this region because cup of excellence, before cup of excellence, we sold all these coffees like commercial coffees, like commodities. And before we start cupping, we found the quality and we started to separate the coffees, and in the last five years we learned a lot from you, from the buyers, a lot of buyers come in this area and we learn a lot, because you tell us what other people are making for specialty coffee in other countries, to keep the quality, drying process, to storage, everything.
>
> COLBY: Have you seen changes since, even since the past five years since specialty coffee has been involved?
>
> ARTURO: (nodding head) Yeah, yeah, yeah.
>
> COLBY: What kind of changes?

ARTURO: For example, in the cupping table, you found five years ago, you found some defects. This year, in all the coffees we cupped, we never found defect. Like mold, like overferment, dirty. Right now, no, it's very clean, and for me the biggest step we make in specialty here is the dry process and the storage process, we changed and this helped in quality.

When a green buyer like Colby has finished meeting with potential farmers and cupping their coffees, the final decision is made about which coffees to purchase. In the case of La Colmena, Verve purchased just over 450 pounds, making it the smallest transaction of the season. Arturo admitted that his farm produces less coffee and at a slower rate, but the quality is high enough to make up for that. Verve paid him an average of $4/pound. But I was curious, of that price, how much does the farmer actually see? For Verve's Honduran coffees, all transactions are brokered through the Beneficio San Vicente, where Arturo and Benjamin work. For other countries, there might be more hands involved before the coffee reaches the exporter, where the coffee is referred to as "Freight on Board," or FOB. The moment the coffee passes the bow of the boat, it transfers hands from the exporter to the importer. Each step of the way, there must be accountability for the freight. The FOB price is the one that is reported by the "C" market, the fair trade certification agencies, and green buyers. So, that $4 that Arturo received is the FOB price. The mill takes that FOB price and scoops out either $.55/lb if the coffee is dry, or $.64 if the mill has to dry the coffee for the producer.

That means that, all told, Arturo walked away with $3.45/lb for his coffee. If it required drying, he'd walk away with $3.36. If you multiply $3.45 times 456 pounds, Arturo's income for this crop was $1,573. By comparison, the "C" market price in May of 2014 was $1.60/lb (International Coffee Organization ico.org). Removing the same $.45/lb, Arturo would have only made $524 dollars for his crop. With direct trade, he is acquiring three times more than commercially traded coffee.

I used the same equation to estimate the differences our other Honduran producers experienced that season. The difference reflects what these producers gained by selling to specialty coffee as opposed to accepting market price.

Name of farmer and farm	(Lbs./coffee)(Market price minus mill surcharge)	Direct Trade Price (Verve paid, minus mill surcharge)	Difference (what farmer gained by selling to specialty coffee)
Arturo Paz La Colmena	(456)(1.15) = 524	(456)(3.45) = 1,573	$1,049
Leonisio Castellon	(2584)(1.15) = 2,971	(2584)(3.42) = 8,837	$5,866
Franklin Madrid La Patepluma	(1064)(1.15) = 1,223	(1064)(3.45) = 3,671	$2,448
Juan Benitez	(1064)(1.15) = 1,223	(1064)(3.45) = 3,671	$2,448
Rodrigo Erazo	(760)(1.15) = 874	(760)(2.70) = 2,052	$1,178
Danilo P.	(608)(1.15) = 699	(608)(2.35) = 1,429	$729

Leonisio Castellon

Juan Benitez

Franklin Madrid

Arturo Paz

Danilo P.

Leonisio’s Family Sorting

Conclusion

Opportunities for the Future

> "This disparity that exists between the coffee-growing world and the coffee-consuming world is rooted in the centuries and remains the true inheritance of 500 years of colonialism. Although no one in today's coffee industry created the existing situation, everyone, including importers, brokers, roasters, retailers, and consumers, are left with this legacy either to perpetuate or address."
>
> Bill Fishbein,
> Founder of Coffee Kids 1992[15]

The risk associated with farming is not quantifiable and measurable like the pecuniary differences I displayed in the last segment. Because coffee has taken root since its colonial conception and embedded itself into the daily lives of billions of people worldwide, there will always be a market and a demand for it. Because coffee only grows in equatorial regions where developing countries are located, the dynamic between growers and buyers will always be haunted and tinged by the remnants of a colonial power differential. As the world continues to be affected by the changes of global warming, droughts and airborne fungi like roya, cash crops like coffee will dwell within that matrix of uncertainty. In our hyper-accelerated post-industrial digital world ruled by the dollar,

[15] Fishbein and Cycon 1992 from *World Coffee and* Tea; cited from "The Rise of Yuppie Coffees and the Reimagination of Class in the United States" by William Roseberry, 1996, in *The Cultural Politics of Food and Eating* edited by Watson and Caldwell

consumers in the materialistic culture of the Global North and America will continue to funnel their funds into brands, technology and goods that they deem worthy, and corporate coffee giants like Starbucks will continue to buy over 600 million pounds of coffee at commercial prices.

Commercial prices are too low for farmers to be able to support their farming and their basic livelihood, and that of their families. Fair Trade offers an alternative to the volatility of the commercial "C" market, yet the criteria for membership in Fair Trade cooperatives is dictated by third party certification agencies which make challenging regimens for farmers to follow and keep up with. Also, as scholars point out, there are internal controversies of rights and fairness that are inextricably linked with the glimmer of hope Fair Trade offers.

Companies like Verve are utilizing an altruistic business approach, wherein their marketing is aimed toward consumer activists who feel as though they are contributing to broader social issues while paying for already desirable items. At times these ideas are merely false fronts with empty truths, capitalizing on the plight of those in developing countries. Other times the business model hinges on a connection with those in the developing world for mutually beneficial outcomes, even though there are costs associated with that dynamic.

For the farmer, there needs to be safety and mitigation for the risks they assume in the unpredictable world of cash crops. For businesses engaging these producers, there needs to be an awareness of the colonial history that imbues their exchanges with memories of injustice and exploitation. Global Northern businesses interested in resource extraction that fuels the coffee industry are obligated to develop business ethics that appreciate the potential plight of their Southern hemisphere counterparts to the point where they implement contracts or support programs that ensure the financial equilibrium of their shared interest, the health of the coffee and its continued success.

Moreover, from the experience I've gained standing on those farms, shaking the hands of the producers that supply Verve, I've learned that humans have a moral imperative to support fellow humans, transcending nefarious backgrounds of colonial mercantilism and envisioning a future where the supply chain becomes more of a partnership, where people in both the Global North and the Global South can enjoy the benefits of a highly lucrative international enterprise.

From here I see various opportunities that consumers and specialty coffee companies can utilize for a future where the colonialism surrounding the coffee supply chain can be addressed. First, as mentioned, specialty coffee companies can implement an insurance program that is built in as a condition of working with a green buyer. If, for any reason, coffee isn't as high quality during a growing season after a relationship has first been instigated, monetary or agricultural resources can be provided as a means of offering the producer a safety net and an advantage to get back on track. Secondly, green buyers can be hired who have proficiency in Spanish or the appropriate African language that producers use as a means of getting on the same level with the producer, as opposed to the less than desirable use of a translator.

Translation is a useful resource, but it keeps a distance between the farmer and the buyer and there might be intentions or subtleties that are lost during translation. Speaking the same language will allow a bridge to form between the two parties, further uniting them and fostering that connection.

Third, programs can be established in cafés to educate consumers on the ethical practices used to purchase coffee, using complete transparency and avoiding one-for-one marketing tactics to entice oblivious spending. The same programs can be implemented in the training of staff so that employees understand the importance of their interfacing with customers as a direct pipeline to farms and coffee production.

It is my hope that I, as an advocate for both farmers and the specialty coffee industry, can work as an ambassador to these causes and maintain what I've learned to apply to my job and transcend the colonial and iniquitous implications of the coffee supply chain to move toward a mutually beneficial future.

References

Anderson, Mark David. *Black and Indigenous: Garifuna Activism and Consumer Culture in Honduras*. Minneapolis: U of Minnesota, 2009. Print.

Booth, John A., Christine J. Wade, and Thomas W. Walker. *Understanding Central America: Global Forces, Rebellion, and Change*. Boulder, CO: Westview, 2006. Print.

CIA World Fact Sheet. *Central Intelligence Agency*. Central Intelligence Agency, 30 Nov. 2010. Web. 05 Apr. 2015.

Clarence-Smith, W. G., and Steven Topik. *The Global Coffee Economy in Africa, Asia and Latin America, 1500-1989*. Cambridge, UK: Cambridge UP, 2003. Print.

Davenport, Jim. "If We Assume: The United States of Starbucks." *If We Assume: The United States of Starbucks*. N.p., 2009. Web. 01 Apr. 2015.

Gold, Jonathon. "La Mill: The Latest Buzz." *LA Weekly*. N.p., 12 Mar. 2008. Web. 02 Apr. 2015.

"The History Of Coffee." - *National Coffee Association*. N.p., n.d. Web. 21 Mar. 2015.

Human Development Reports. *Human Development Reports*. N.p., n.d. Web. 05 Apr. 2015.

Žižek, Slavoj. "First as Comedy, Then as Farce." Royal Society for the Encouragement of Arts, Manufactures and Commerce (RSA). London. *Rsa.org*. Web.

IHCAFE - Instituto Hondureño Del Café. *IHCAFE - Instituto Hondureño Del Café*. N.p., n.d. Web. 31 Mar. 2015.

"International Coffee Organization." *International Coffee Organization*. N.p., n.d. Web. 05 Apr. 2015.

Jaffee, Daniel. *Brewing Justice: Fair Trade Coffee, Sustainability, and Survival*. Berkeley: U of California, 2007. Print.

Lyon, Sarah, and Mark Moberg. *Fair Trade and Social Justice: Global Ethnographies*. New York: New York UP, 2010. Print.

Mintz, Sidney W. "Enduring Substances, Trying Theories: The Caribbean Region as Oikoumene." *The Journal of the Royal Anthropological Institute* 2.2 (1996): 289.

Mintz, Sidney Wilfred. *Sweetness and Power: The Place of Sugar in Modern History*. New York, NY: Viking, 1985. Print.

Moodie, Megan. "Microfinance and the Gender of Risk: The Case of Kiva.org." *Signs* 38.2 (2013): 279-302.

"New Impact Report Released." *Fairtrade International*. N.p., n.d. Web. 05 Apr. 2015.

Reichman, Daniel R. *The Broken Village: Coffee, Migration, and Globalization in Honduras*. Ithaca: ILR, 2011. Print.

"Rural Poverty Portal." *Rural Poverty Portal*. N.p., n.d. Web. 05 Apr. 2015.

Sen, Debarati, and Sarasij Majumder. "Fair Trade and Fair Trade Certification of Food and Agricultural Commodities: Promises, Pitfalls, and Possibilities." *Environment and Society: Advances in Research* 2.1 (2011): 29-47. Web.

Smith, Julia. "The Search for Sustainable Markets: The Promise and Failures of Fair Trade." *Culture & Agriculture* 29.2 (2007): 89-99.

"Specialty Coffee Association of America." *Specialty Coffee Association of America*. N.p., n.d. Web. 15 Feb. 2015.

Tsing, Anna. "Supply Chains and the Human Condition." *Rethinking Marxism* 21.2 (2009): 148-76. Web.

Watson, James L., and Melissa L. Caldwell. The Cultural Politics of Food and Eating: A Reader. Malden, MA: Blackwell Pub., 2005. Print.

Weissman, Michaele. *God in a Cup: The Obsessive Quest for the Perfect Coffee*. Hoboken, NJ: J. Wiley, 2008. Print.

West, Paige. *From Modern Production to Imagined Primitive: The Social World of Coffee from*
Papua New Guinea. Durham, NC: Duke UP, 2012. Print

Acknowledgements

This thesis would not be possible without the support and guidance of the many people who have touched my life academically, professionally and personally. First, I want to thank Ted Hamilton and Paula Clarke for their intense, at times grueling, profoundly knowledgeable, and kind preparation at Columbia College in Sonora, California that all lead me to where I am today and the woman that I have become. Without undergoing that high demand-high support environment (eight times over) I would have never chosen anthropology and I would have never realized how hard I could work at how much those resilience promoting opportunities would grant me. What you've taught me will stay with me forever.

To my faculty advisor, Megan Moodie. Because of your refusal to settle for anything less than a thorough and succinct paper, I was forced to go out of my comfort zone and take a different perspective on an issue which can be hard to fully comprehend, since I am so close to it. I believe it's in those moments of discomfort and doubt when true transformation begins. We are asked to transcend preconceived notions and break through barriers. Thank you for your guidance along the way.

To my family, friends, coworkers and Morgan. Thank you for being psyched and coaxing me along, even when my heels dragged.

Without the support of Verve Coffee Roasters and its cofounder himself, Colby Barr, I would have written a paper that only fantasized and assumed what it's like to be at origin. Because you believed in me and recognized my passion and personal initiative I was able to manifest this paper, but more than that it became an experience that will enrich my personal and professional life for years to come. Now as I proudly stand behind that counter at the original 41st avenue café, I can relate to customers, regulars, friends and coworkers alike how important what we do is and how ardently I believe in what we're doing. I can't wait to see where we go from here.

Can't stop. Won't stop.

Katie Slocum

12090703R00052

Printed in Germany
by Amazon Distribution
GmbH, Leipzig